BUILDING SCALABLE FLASK APIs

A Practical Guide to Design, Implementation, and Deployment

Saul E. Sanchez

TABLE OF CONTENTS

CONCLUSION
KEY TAKEAWAYS
FUTURE TRENDS IN API DEVELOPMENT
ENCOURAGING FURTHER EXPLORATION AND LEARNING

INTRODUCTION

WHAT IS AN API?

API stands for **Application Programming Interface.** In simpler terms, it's a set of rules and specifications that software programs can follow to communicate with each other. It acts as a middleman, allowing different applications to interact and exchange data.

Think of an API as a waiter in a restaurant:
- The customer (application): Orders food (sends requests).
- The waiter (API): Takes the order to the kitchen (sends the request to the server).
- The kitchen (server): Prepares the food (processes the request).
- The waiter (API): Brings the food back to the customer (sends the response).

Key Components of an API:
- Endpoint: A specific address or URL where requests are sent.
- Request: The data sent to the API, often in a specific format like JSON or XML.
- Response: The data returned by the API, usually in a similar format to the request.

Types of APIs:
- Public APIs: Open to the public, often used for building third-party applications.
- Private APIs:Used internally within an organization.
- Partner APIs: Shared between specific organizations or partners.

Common Use Cases of APIs:
- Social Media Integration: Allowing apps to share content to platforms like Facebook and Twitter.

- Payment Processing: Facilitating secure online payments.
- Data Exchange: Sharing data between different systems and applications.
- Map Services: Providing maps and location-based services.
- Weather Data: Accessing real-time weather information.

WHY USE FLASK FOR API DEVELOPMENT?

Flask is a popular Python web framework that's particularly well-suited for building APIs. **WHY?**

Simplicity and Flexibility
- Minimalistic Framework: Flask offers a straightforward approach to web development, making it easy to learn and use.
- Customizability: You have the freedom to structure your applications as you see fit, without being constrained by rigid conventions.

Rapid Development
- Quick Prototyping: Flask's simplicity allows for rapid development and iteration.
- Built-in Development Server: Easily test your API locally without complex setup.

Strong Community and Ecosystem
- Extensive Documentation: Comprehensive official documentation and a wealth of community resources.
- Large Ecosystem: A wide range of extensions and libraries to enhance your API development.

RESTful API Support
- Built-in Tools: Flask provides tools for handling HTTP requests and responses, making it easy to build RESTful APIs.
- Flexible Routing: Design clean and intuitive API endpoints.

Integration with Other Technologies
- Compatibility: Seamlessly integrate with other technologies like databases (SQLAlchemy), template engines (Jinja2), and front-end frameworks (React, Vue).

Ideal for Microservices
- Lightweight: Flask's minimal footprint makes it perfect for building microservices.
- Scalability: Easily scale your API to handle increasing traffic and data loads.

OVERVIEW OF THE BOOK'S STRUCTURE

This book is designed to guide you through a comprehensive journey of API development using Flask. We'll cover everything from foundational concepts to advanced techniques.

Here's a breakdown of what you can expect:

Part I: Flask Fundamentals
- Setting the Stage: We'll start by setting up your development environment and introducing you to the core concepts of Flask.
- Building Blocks: Learn the fundamentals of routing, request handling, templates, and forms.
- Your First Flask App: Put your knowledge into practice by building a simple Flask application.

Part II: API Design and Development
- RESTful Principles: Understand the principles of RESTful API design, including HTTP methods and status codes.
- Designing APIs with Flask: Learn how to design efficient and user-friendly API endpoints.

- Implementing Endpoints: Dive into the practical aspects of handling requests, processing data, and returning responses.
- Advanced Features: Explore advanced techniques like authentication, authorization, pagination, and websockets.

Part III: Testing, Debugging, and Deployment

- Ensuring Quality: Learn how to test your API thoroughly using unit and integration tests.
- Troubleshooting: Discover effective debugging techniques to identify and fix issues.
- Deploying Your API: Deploy your API to production environments, ensuring scalability and reliability.

Part IV: Advanced Topics and Best Practices

- API Versioning: Strategically manage API versions to accommodate changes.
- Performance Optimization: Fine-tune your API for optimal performance.
- Security Best Practices: Protect your API from vulnerabilities and attacks.
- API Documentation: Create clear and concise documentation for your API.

PART I: FLASK FUNDAMENTALS

SETTING UP A FLASK DEVELOPMENT ENVIRONMENT

Installation
- Installing Python: Ensure you have Python installed on your system. You can download the latest version from the official Python website.
- Installing Flask: Use pip, the package installer for Python, to install Flask:
    Bash

```bash
pip install Flask
```

Creating a Basic Flask Application
- Create a New Python File: Let's name it `app.py`.
- Import the Flask Class:
    python

```python
from flask import Flask
```

- Create a Flask App Instance:
    python

```python
app = Flask(__name__)
```

- Define a Route and a Function:
    python

```python
@app.route('/')
def hello_world():
  return 'Hello, World!'
```

- Run the Application:

Bash

```
python app.py
```

Understanding the Code:
`Flask(__name__)`: Creates a Flask application instance.
`@app.route('/')`: Defines a route, in this case, the root URL (`/`).
`def hello_world():`: Defines a function that returns the response for the route.

Additional Tips:
- Virtual Environments: Use virtual environments to isolate project dependencies.
- Text Editor or IDE: Choose a suitable code editor like Visual Studio Code or PyCharm.
- Flask Extensions: Explore various Flask extensions to enhance your application's functionality.

CORE CONCEPTS OF FLASK

Routes and Request Handling
- Routing: Flask uses a simple and intuitive routing system to map URLs to Python functions

python

```python
@app.route('/users/<username>')
def greet_user(username):
    return f"Hello, {username}!"
```

This route will match URLs like `/users/alice` and `/users/bob`.

- Request Handling: Flask provides various tools to work with incoming requests:

- Request Object: Access information about the incoming request, such as headers, cookies, and form data.
- Response Object: Create and customize HTTP responses, including setting status codes, headers, and cookies.

Templates and Static Files
- Templates: Flask uses Jinja2 as a powerful templating engine. Templates allow you to dynamically generate HTML content.

python

```python
@app.route('/profile/<username>')
def profile(username):
    return                              render_template('profile.html',
username=username)
```

- Static Files: You can serve static files like images, CSS, and JavaScript. Flask has a built-in mechanism to handle static files.

Forms and Sessions
- Forms: Flask-WTForms provides a way to create and validate HTML forms.
- Sessions: Flask-Session allows you to maintain user sessions, storing information across multiple requests.

BUILDING A BASIC FLASK APPLICATION

Simple Web Application
Let's build a simple web application that displays a welcome message and a form to collect user input.

1. Project Setup:
- Create a new project directory.
- Create a Python file named `app.py`.

2. Import Necessary Modules:
python

```python
from flask import Flask, render_template, request
```

3. Create a Flask App Instance:
python

```python
app = Flask(__name__)
```

4. Define a Route for the Home Page:
python

```python
@app.route('/')
def index():
    return render_template('index.html')
```

5. Create the `index.html` Template:
html

```html
<!DOCTYPE html>
<html>
<head>
  <title>Welcome</title>
</head>
<body>
  <h1>Welcome to My Flask App</h1>
  <form method="POST" action="/greet">
    <label for="name">Name:</label>
    <input type="text" id="name" name="name">
    <input type="submit" value="Greet Me">
  </form>
</body>
```

```
</html>
```

6. Define a Route to Handle Form Submissions:
python
```python
@app.route('/greet', methods=['POST'])
def greet():
    name = request.form['name']
    return render_template('greet.html', name=name)
```

7. Create the `greet.html` Template:
html
```html
<!DOCTYPE html>
<html>
<head>
  <title>Greeting</title>
</head>
<body>
  <h1>Hello, {{ name }}!</h1>
</body>
</html>
```

8. Run the Application:
Bash

```bash
python app.py
```

How it Works:
- When a user visits the root URL (`/`), the `index` function is called.
- The `index` function renders the `index.html` template.
- When the user submits the form, the `greet` function is called.
- The `greet` function extracts the `name` from the form data.

- The `greet` function renders the `greet.html` template, passing the `name` as a template variable.

PART II: API DESIGN AND DEVELOPMENT

RESTful API PRINCIPLES

Understanding RESTful APIs
A RESTful API is an application programming interface that conforms to the architectural style of REST (Representational State Transfer). It's designed to be simple, scalable, and maintainable.

Key Principles of RESTful APIs:
- Client-Server Architecture: The client and server are separate entities that communicate over HTTP.
- Statelessness: Each request from the client must contain all the information necessary to understand and process the request.
- Cacheability: Responses can be cached to improve performance.
- Uniform Interface: A uniform set of interfaces (URLs, methods, and data formats) should be used.
- Layered System: The architecture can be layered, allowing for intermediaries like load balancers and proxies.

HTTP Methods in RESTful APIs:
GET: Retrieves resources.
POST: Creates new resources.
PUT: Updates existing resources.
DELETE: Deletes resources.

Example of a RESTful API:
Let's consider a simple blog API:
GET /posts: Retrieves a list of all posts.
GET /posts/<id>: Retrieves a specific post by ID.
POST /posts: Creates a new post.

PUT /posts/<id>: Updates an existing post.
DELETE /posts/<id>: Deletes a post.

DESIGNING APIs WITH FLASK

Routing and URL Design
- Defining Routes: Use the `@app.route()` decorator to define routes and their corresponding functions.

python
```
@app.route('/users')
def get_users():
    # ...
```

- URL Parameters: Use `<variable_name>` to capture dynamic segments in URLs.

python
```
@app.route('/users/<username>')
def get_user(username):
    # ...
```

- HTTP Methods: Specify the allowed HTTP methods for a route using the `methods` argument.

python
```
@app.route('/users', methods=['POST'])
def create_user():
    # ...
```

Request Parameters and Query Strings
Request Parameters: Extract parameters from the URL using the `args` attribute of the `request` object.

python

```python
@app.route('/users/<username>')
def get_user(username):
    page = request.args.get('page', 1, type=int)
    # ...
```

- Query Strings: Parse query parameters using the `request.args` dictionary.

python
```python
@app.route('/search')
def search():
    query = request.args.get('q')
    # ...
```

Error Handling and Exception Handling

- Error Handling: Use HTTP status codes to indicate success or failure.

python
```python
@app.route('/users/<username>')
def get_user(username):
    # ...
    if user is None:
        return 'User not found', 404
```

- Exception Handling: Use `try-except` blocks to handle exceptions.

python
```python
@app.route('/users/<username>')
def get_user(username):
    try:
        # ...
    except DatabaseError:
        return 'Database error', 500
```

IMPLEMENTING API ENDPOINTS

Handling HTTP Requests

- Request Object: Flask provides a `request` object to access information about the incoming request, including:
- `request.args`: Query parameters
- `request.form`: Form data
- `request.json`: JSON data
- `request.headers`: HTTP headers
- `request.method`: HTTP method (GET, POST, PUT, DELETE, etc.)

Processing Request Data

- Parsing Request Data: Use appropriate methods to parse request data based on the content type:
- `request.args.get()` for query parameters
- `request.form.get()` for form data
- `request.json` for JSON data
- Validating Input Data: Use validation libraries like `Werkzeug` or custom validation logic to ensure data integrity.

Returning Responses

- JSON Responses: Use the `jsonify()` function to return JSON responses.

```python
@app.route('/users')
def get_users():
    users = [
        {'id': 1, 'name': 'Alice'},
        {'id': 2, 'name': 'Bob'}
    ]
    return jsonify(users)
```

- Custom Responses: Create custom responses by setting status codes and headers.

```python
@app.route('/users/<username>')
def get_user(username):
    # ...
    if user is None:
```

```
    return 'User not found', 404
```

Example: A Simple Blog API
Let's create a basic blog API with endpoints to create, read, update, and delete blog posts:

```python
from flask import Flask, jsonify, request

app = Flask(__name__)

posts = [
    {'id': 1, 'title': 'Post 1', 'content': 'Content 1'},
    {'id': 2, 'title': 'Post 2', 'content': 'Content 2'}
]

@app.route('/posts', methods=['GET'])
def get_posts():
    return jsonify(posts)

@app.route('/posts/<int:post_id>', methods=['GET'])
def get_post(post_id):
    post = next((p for p in posts if p['id'] == post_id), None)
    if post:
        return jsonify(post)
    else:
        return 'Post not found', 404

# ... (Implement POST, PUT, DELETE endpoints)
```

ADVANCED API FEATURES

Authentication and Authorization

- Basic Authentication: Simple authentication mechanism using HTTP Basic Authentication.
- Token-Based Authentication: Using tokens (e.g., JWT) to authenticate users.
- OAuth: A widely used authorization framework for delegating access to resources.

Pagination and Filtering
- Pagination: Implement pagination to handle large datasets and improve performance.
- Filtering: Allow users to filter results based on specific criteria.

WebSockets for Real-time Communication
- Flask-SocketIO: Use this extension to enable real-time communication between the server and clients.
- Real-time Features: Build features like chat applications, notifications, and live updates.

API Versioning and Migration
- URL-Based Versioning: Use different URL prefixes for different API versions.
- Header-Based Versioning: Use a custom HTTP header to specify the API version.
- Content Negotiation: Use content negotiation to select the appropriate API version based on the client's capabilities.

Effective Communication in API Development

Clear and concise communication is essential for successful API development. Here are some key aspects to consider:

1. API Documentation
- Swagger UI: A powerful tool for generating interactive API documentation.
- OpenAPI Specification: A standardized format for describing RESTful APIs.

- Documentation Standards: Adhere to clear documentation standards to ensure consistency.

2. Collaboration and Teamwork
- Version Control: Use Git or other version control systems to track changes and collaborate with team members.
- Code Reviews: Conduct regular code reviews to maintain code quality and identify potential issues.
- Agile Methodologies: Employ Agile methodologies like Scrum or Kanban for efficient project management.

3. API Design and Governance
- API Design Guidelines: Establish guidelines for API design, including naming conventions, error handling, and security best practices.
- API Governance: Implement a governance process to manage API lifecycle, versioning, and deprecation.
- API Security: Prioritize API security by implementing measures like authentication, authorization, and data encryption.

4. Communication with Stakeholders
- Clear Communication: Communicate effectively with stakeholders, including developers, product managers, and business analysts.
- Regular Updates: Provide regular updates on project progress, challenges, and solutions.
- Feedback Mechanisms: Encourage feedback from stakeholders to improve the API design and development process.

By following these communication best practices, you can ensure that your API development projects are successful and meet the needs of your users.

PART III: API TESTING AND DEBUGGING

TESTING FLASK APIs

Ensuring API Quality

Testing is a crucial step in the API development process. It helps identify and fix bugs, improve code quality, and ensure that the API functions as expected.

Types of API Tests:

1. Unit Tests:
- Test individual units of code in isolation.
- Use a testing framework like `pytest` to write unit tests.
- Focus on testing small functions and methods.

2. Integration Tests:
- Test how different components of the API interact with each other.
- Simulate HTTP requests to the API endpoints.
- Use tools like `requests` or `pytest-flask` to write integration tests.

3. End-to-End Tests:
- Test the entire API workflow, from user input to server response.
- Use tools like `Selenium` or `Playwright` to automate browser interactions.

Testing Tools and Frameworks:
- **pytest:** A powerful and flexible testing framework for Python.
- **requests:** A library for making HTTP requests.
- **pytest-flask:** A pytest plugin for testing Flask applications.
- **unittest:** Python's built-in unit testing framework.
- **Selenium:** A browser automation tool for testing web applications.
- **Playwright:** A modern automation library for web browsers.

Example of a Unit Test:

python
import pytest

```python
from app import app

def test_hello_world():
    with app.test_client() as client:
        response = client.get('/')
        assert response.status_code == 200
        assert response.data == b'Hello, World!'
```

Example of an Integration Test:

```python
import requests

def test_get_posts():
    response = requests.get('http://127.0.0.1:5000/posts')
    assert response.status_code == 200
    assert len(response.json()) > 0
```

By writing comprehensive tests, you can ensure the quality and reliability of your Flask APIs.

DEBUGGING FLASK APIs

Identifying and Resolving Issues
Debugging is an essential skill for any developer. When building APIs with Flask, it's crucial to have effective debugging techniques to identify and fix issues.

Common Debugging Techniques:

1. Print Statements:
- Use `print()` statements to log variables and intermediate results.
- While simple, this can be helpful for basic debugging.

2. Flask's Built-in Debugger:

- Activate the debugger by setting the `DEBUG` environment variable to `True`.
- This will provide a web interface for debugging, including variable inspection and code execution.

3. Logging:

- Use Python's built-in `logging` module to log messages at different levels (DEBUG, INFO, WARNING, ERROR).
- Configure logging to write logs to a file or to the console.

Example:

```python
import logging

app.logger.setLevel(logging.DEBUG)
app.logger.debug('Debugging message')
```

4. Profiling:

- Use profiling tools to identify performance bottlenecks in your code.
- Tools like `cProfile` and `pyinstrument` can help you profile your Flask application.

5. Third-Party Debugging Tools:

- Consider using advanced debugging tools like `pdb` (Python Debugger) or `PyCharm`'s debugger for more granular control.

Tips for Effective Debugging:

- Break Down the Problem: Divide the problem into smaller, more manageable parts.
- Isolate the Issue: Try to isolate the specific code that is causing the problem.
- Use a Systematic Approach: Follow a structured approach to debugging, such as the scientific method.

- Leverage Debugging Tools: Utilize debugging tools to inspect variables, step through code, and analyze logs.
- Learn from Errors: Analyze error messages and stack traces to gain insights into the root cause of the problem.

By mastering these debugging techniques, you'll be well-equipped to troubleshoot and resolve issues in your Flask APIs.

OPTIMIZING FLASK APIs

Improving Performance and Scalability
Optimizing your Flask API is crucial for delivering a high-performance and scalable application. Here are some key techniques to consider:

1. Database Optimization
- Efficient Query Design: Write efficient SQL queries to minimize database load.
- Database Indexing: Create appropriate indexes to speed up query execution.
- Connection Pooling: Use connection pooling to reduce the overhead of establishing database connections.

2. Caching
- HTTP Caching: Use HTTP caching headers to instruct browsers and CDNs to cache responses.
- Database Caching: Cache frequently accessed data in memory or a dedicated cache server.

3. Asynchronous Programming
- Asynchronous Frameworks: Consider using asynchronous frameworks like Flask-Async or Quart.
- Asyncio: Leverage asynchronous programming with the `asyncio` library.

4. Code Optimization

- Profiling: Use profiling tools to identify performance bottlenecks.
- Optimize Algorithms: Choose efficient algorithms and data structures.
- Minimize Database Queries: Reduce the number of database queries by using caching and batch processing.
- Template Optimization: Optimize template rendering by minimizing template complexity and using template caching.

5. Server Configuration

- Load Balancing: Distribute traffic across multiple servers to improve scalability.
- Caching Servers: Use caching servers to reduce server load.
- CDN: Utilize a Content Delivery Network to improve website performance and reduce server load.

By applying these optimization techniques, you can significantly improve the performance and scalability of your Flask API.

PART IV: API DEPLOYMENT AND SECURITY

DEPLOYING FLASK APIs

Deploying Your API to Production

Once you've developed and tested your Flask API, the next step is to deploy it to a production environment. This involves making your API accessible to the public or a specific audience.

1. Choosing a Deployment Platform

Cloud Platforms:

- Heroku: A popular platform for deploying web applications, including Flask apps.
- AWS: Offers a wide range of services, including EC2 instances, Elastic Beanstalk, and Lambda functions.
- Google Cloud Platform (GCP): Provides App Engine, Compute Engine, and other services for deploying Flask apps.

Self-Hosted Servers:

- DigitalOcean: A cloud hosting provider that offers virtual servers.
- Linode: Another cloud hosting provider with similar offerings.

2. Deployment Process

Packaging Your Application:

- Create a deployment package, such as a Docker image or a ZIP file.

Configuring the Environment

- Set up the necessary environment variables, such as database credentials and API keys.

Deploying to the Platform:

- Follow the platform's specific instructions to deploy your application.
- This may involve using a command-line tool, a web interface, or a configuration file.

Configuring the Web Server:

- Set up a web server like Nginx or Apache to handle incoming requests and forward them to your Flask app.
- Monitoring and Logging:

Implement monitoring tools to track your API's performance and health.
- Set up logging to record errors, warnings, and other important information.

3. Considerations for Production Deployment
- Security: Implement security measures like HTTPS, input validation, and rate limiting.
- Performance: Optimize your application for performance, especially if you expect high traffic.
- Scalability: Design your infrastructure to handle increasing loads.
- Monitoring: Use monitoring tools to track your API's health and performance.
- Error Handling: Implement robust error handling and logging.

By following these steps and considering the key factors, you can successfully deploy your Flask API to production.

API SECURITY

Protecting Your API and User Data
API security is crucial to protect your application and user data from potential threats. Here are some essential security best practices:

1. Authentication and Authorization
- HTTP Basic Authentication: A simple authentication scheme that sends credentials in the request header.
- Token-Based Authentication: Uses tokens (e.g., JWT) to authenticate users.
- OAuth 2.0: A popular authorization framework for delegating access to resources.
- Role-Based Access Control (RBAC): Restrict access to resources based on user roles and permissions.

2. Input Validation and Sanitization

- Input Validation: Validate user input to prevent malicious attacks like SQL injection and cross-site scripting (XSS).
- Sanitization: Clean and sanitize user input to remove harmful characters.

3. Data Encryption
- Encrypt Sensitive Data: Encrypt sensitive data like passwords and credit card information using strong encryption algorithms.
- Secure Data Transmission: Use HTTPS to encrypt communication between the client and server.

4. Rate Limiting
- Prevent Abuse: Implement rate limiting to limit the number of requests a client can make within a certain time period.

5. Security Headers
- Set Security Headers: Use security headers like `Content-Security-Policy` and `X-Frame-Options` to protect against attacks.

6. Regular Security Audits
- Penetration Testing: Conduct regular penetration testing to identify vulnerabilities.
- Security Reviews: Conduct regular security reviews of your code and infrastructure.

7. Secure Development Practices
- Keep Dependencies Updated: Keep your dependencies up-to-date to address security vulnerabilities.
- Secure Coding Practices: Follow secure coding practices to avoid common vulnerabilities.
- Regular Security Training: Train your development team on security best practices.

By following these security best practices, you can significantly enhance the security of your Flask API and protect your users' data.

PART V: ADVANCED TOPICS AND BEST PRACTICES

API VERSIONING AND MIGRATION STRATEGIES

As your API evolves, you may need to introduce new features or change existing functionality. API versioning is a strategy to manage these changes while maintaining compatibility with older clients.

Common Versioning Strategies:

1. URL-Based Versioning:
- Assign different URL prefixes or suffixes to different API versions.
- Example: `/v1/users`, `/v2/users`

2. Header-Based Versioning:
- Use a custom HTTP header to specify the API version.
- Example: `X-API-Version: 2`

3. Content Negotiation:
- Use content negotiation to select the appropriate API version based on the client's capabilities.

Migration Strategies:
- Gradual Rollout: Gradually introduce new features in a non-breaking way.
- Deprecation Period: Provide a deprecation period for older API versions.
- Redesign and Rebuild: For major changes, consider a complete redesign and rebuild of your API.

API PERFORMANCE OPTIMIZATION

Optimizing API performance is crucial for delivering a seamless user experience. Here are some key techniques:

- Efficient Query Design: Write optimized SQL queries to minimize database load.
- Caching: Implement caching strategies to reduce database queries and improve response times.
- Asynchronous Programming: Use asynchronous programming techniques to handle multiple requests concurrently.
- Minification and Compression: Minimize and compress your API responses to reduce bandwidth usage.
- Load Balancing: Distribute traffic across multiple servers to improve scalability.
- Profiling: Use profiling tools to identify performance bottlenecks.

API MONITORING AND LOGGING

Monitoring and logging are essential for understanding your API's health and performance.

Key Monitoring Metrics:
- Response Time:Average response time of API requests.
- Error Rate: Percentage of requests that result in errors.
- Throughput: Number of requests processed per unit of time.
- Resource Utilization: CPU, memory, and disk usage.

Logging Best Practices:
- Log Important Events: Log errors, warnings, and informational messages.
- Structured Logging: Use structured logging formats (e.g., JSON) for easier parsing and analysis.
- Centralized Logging: Use a centralized logging system like ELK Stack to collect and analyze logs.

API SECURITY BEST PRACTICES

In addition to the security measures discussed earlier, consider these advanced best practices:

- Secure Coding Practices: Follow secure coding guidelines to minimize vulnerabilities.
- Input Validation and Sanitization: Validate and sanitize all user input to prevent attacks like SQL injection and XSS.
- Secure Configuration Management: Protect sensitive information like API keys and database passwords.
- Regular Security Audits: Conduct regular security audits to identify and address vulnerabilities.
- Incident Response Plan: Have a plan in place to respond to security incidents.

API DOCUMENTATION STANDARDS (Swagger, OpenAPI)

Clear and comprehensive API documentation is essential for developers to understand and use your API.

Swagger UI: A powerful tool for generating interactive API documentation.

OpenAPI Specification: A standardized format for describing RESTful APIs.

Documentation Best Practices:
- Use clear and concise language.
- Provide examples and code snippets.
- Include detailed error codes and responses.
- Keep documentation up-to-date.

API DESIGN PATTERNS (REST, GraphQL)

RESTful API Design

REST (Representational State Transfer) is a popular architectural style for building APIs. Key principles of RESTful API design include:

- Client-Server Architecture: Clear separation of concerns between clients and servers.
- Statelessness: Each request from the client must contain all the necessary information.
- Cacheability: Responses can be cached to improve performance.
- Uniform Interface: A consistent set of interfaces for resources.

GraphQL API Design

GraphQL is a query language for APIs that provides a more flexible and efficient way to fetch data. Key features of GraphQL include:

- Strong Typing: Ensures data consistency and reduces errors.
- Introspection: Allows clients to discover the available API schema.
- Efficient Data Fetching: Clients can precisely request the data they need minimizing over-fetching.

Choosing the Right Design Pattern:

- REST: Suitable for simple APIs that expose a fixed set of resources.
- GraphQL: Ideal for complex APIs with many interconnected data points and flexible query requirements.

By understanding these API design patterns, you can build well-structured maintainable, and efficient APIs.

CONCLUSION

KEY TAKEAWAYS

In this book, we've explored the fundamentals of Flask API development, from setting up a development environment to deploying and securing production-grade APIs. Key takeaways include:

- Flask's Simplicity: Flask provides a streamlined and flexible framework for building APIs.
- RESTful Principles: Adhering to REST principles leads to well-structured and scalable APIs.
- API Design Best Practices: Design APIs with clear endpoints, meaningful HTTP methods, and appropriate data formats.
- Testing and Debugging: Thorough testing and effective debugging techniques are essential for API quality.
- Deployment and Security:Deploy your API to production environments and implement robust security measures.
- Advanced Topics: Explore advanced techniques like API versioning, performance optimization, and real-time communication.

FUTURE TRENDS IN API DEVELOPMENT

The API landscape continues to evolve rapidly. Here are some emerging trends:

- Serverless Architecture: Building APIs without managing servers.
- GraphQL: A powerful query language for APIs.
- gRPC: A high-performance, efficient RPC framework.
- API Security and Privacy: Increasing focus on data privacy and security.
- AI and Machine Learning-Powered APIs: Leveraging AI and ML to enhance API capabilities.

ENCOURAGING FURTHER EXPLORATION AND LEARNING

This book has provided a solid foundation in Flask API development. To continue your learning journey, consider exploring the following:

- Advanced Flask Features: Dive deeper into Flask's capabilities and extensions.
- Cloud-Native Development: Learn about cloud-native principles and practices.
- Microservices Architecture: Build scalable and modular API-driven applications.
- API Security Best Practices: Stay up-to-date with the latest security trends and techniques.
- Open-Source API Projects: Contribute to open-source API projects to gain practical experience.

By staying curious and embracing new technologies, you can continue to build innovative and impactful APIs.

The world of APIs is constantly evolving, and staying updated with the latest trends and technologies is crucial.

Happy Coding!